More Professional Tools

SWAT TEAM
TOOLS

ANDERS HANSON

Consulting Editor, Diane Craig, M.A./Reading Specialist

A Division of ABDO
ABDO
Publishing Company

visit us at www.abdopublishing.com

Published by ABDO Publishing Company, a division of ABDO,
P.O. Box 398166, Minneapolis, Minnesota 55439. Copyright © 2014
by Abdo Consulting Group, Inc. International copyrights reserved in all
countries. No part of this book may be reproduced in any form without
written permission from the publisher. Super SandCastle™
is a trademark and logo of ABDO Publishing Company.

Printed in the United States of America,
North Mankato, Minnesota
102013
012014

 PRINTED ON RECYCLED PAPER

Editor: Liz Salzmann
Content Developer: Nancy Tuminelly
Photo Credits: Shutterstock

Library of Congress Cataloging-in-Publication Data

Hanson, Anders, 1980-
  Swat team tools / Anders Hanson.
    pages cm -- (More professional tools)
  Audience: Age 5-10.
  ISBN 978-1-62403-076-5
  1. Police--Special weapons and tactics units--Juvenile literature. I. Title.
  HV8080.S64H36 2014
  363.2'3--dc23
                  2013022423

Super SandCastle™ books are created by a team of professional
educators, reading specialists, and content developers around five
essential components—phonemic awareness, phonics, vocabulary,
text comprehension, and fluency—to assist young readers as they
develop reading skills and strategies and increase their general
knowledge. All books are written, reviewed, and leveled for guided
reading, early reading intervention, and Accelerated Reader®
programs for use in shared, guided, and independent reading and
writing activities to support a balanced approach to literacy
instruction.

CONTENTS

MEET A SWAT OFFICER!

WHAT DOES SWAT MEAN?

SWAT stands for special weapons and **tactics**.

WHAT DOES A SWAT OFFICER DO?

SWAT team members are police officers with special training. They deal with **violent**, armed criminals.

WHY DO SWAT OFFICERS NEED TOOLS?

Tools help SWAT officers protect themselves, get to crime scenes, and stop criminals.

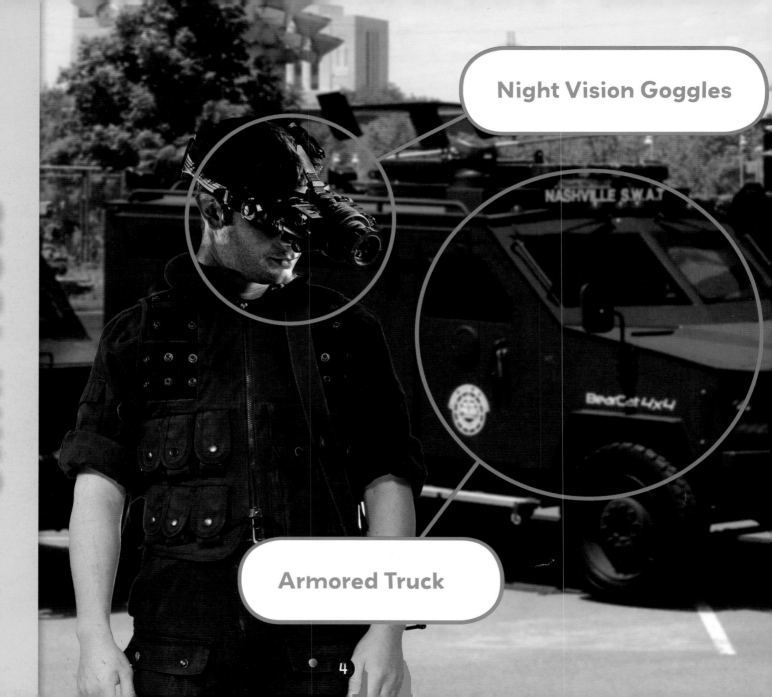

SWAT TOOLS

Night Vision Goggles

NASHVILLE S.W.A.T

BearCat 4x4

Armored Truck

4

BODY ARMOR

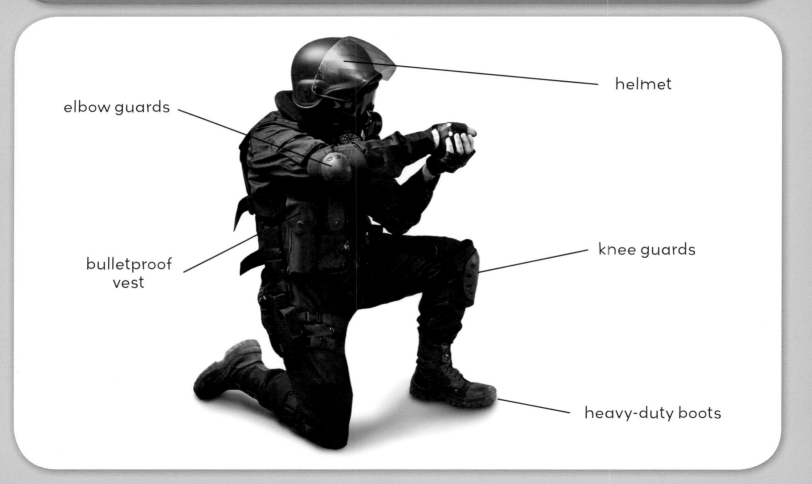

helmet

elbow guards

bulletproof
vest

knee guards

heavy-duty boots

Body armor protects SWAT officers.

SWAT officers wear protective clothing. It's called body armor.

Body armor usually includes a helmet, a **bulletproof** vest, elbow and knee guards, and heavy-duty boots.

SWAT officers Logan and Eli wear helmets. The helmets protect their heads from gunshots.

SWAT officer Nick is wearing a **bulletproof** vest.
The vest protects his chest and back.

ARMORED TRUCK

bulletproof windows

flashing lights

hatch

steel door with bulletproof window and gun port

Armored trucks carry and protect SWAT teams.

Armored trucks take SWAT teams and tools to crime scenes.

Armored trucks also offer protection. SWAT officers can shoot through small holes in the truck. They are called gun ports.

Many armored trucks have hatches on top. An officer can stand in the hatch and shoot in any direction.

The SWAT team practices using an armored truck for cover. The bulletproof truck protects them from gunfire.

NIGHT VISION GOGGLES

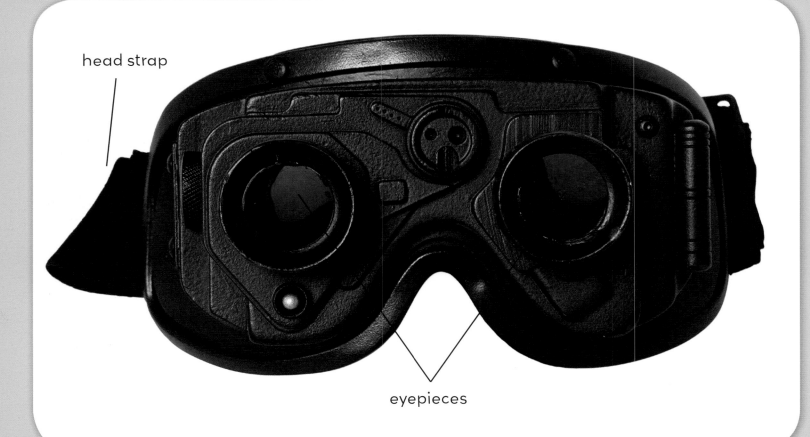

head strap

eyepieces

SWAT officers use night vision goggles to see in the dark.

Many crimes happen at night. It is hard to see what's going on. Night vision goggles help SWAT officers see better.

Night vision goggles have a special tube. It collects light. It makes **invisible** light visible.

Officer Justin looks through night vision goggles. They are heavy. The straps fit around his head to hold them on.

Two SWAT officers use a boat at night. They look green through night vision goggles.

CLIMBING GEAR

SWAT teams use climbing gear to secretly enter buildings.

Climbing gear helps SWAT teams enter buildings through windows and rooftops. They try to surprise any **suspects** inside.

Climbing gear includes ropes, harnesses, and **carabiners.**

Harnesses fit around the officers' waists. They are attached to ropes. The ropes hang from the roof.

Using ropes to climb down a building is called **rappelling**. SWAT officer John is learning how to rappel.

MATCH THE WORDS TO THE PICTURES!

The answers are on the bottom of the page.

MATCH GAME

1. climbing gear

a.

2. body armor

b.

3. night vision goggles

c.

4. armored truck

d.

TEST YOUR TOOL KNOWLEDGE!

The answers are on the bottom of the page.

1.

Body armor does not include a helmet.

TRUE OR FALSE?

2.

Armored trucks have gun ports.

TRUE OR FALSE?

3.

Night vision goggles make things look green.

TRUE OR FALSE?

4.

Harnesses fit around an officer's arms.

TRUE OR FALSE?

TOOL QUIZ

attach – to join or connect.

bulletproof – able to stop objects fired from guns from passing through.

carabiner – a metal ring with a hinge that is used to connect climbing ropes and harnesses.

helicopter – an aircraft that has large rotating blades on top instead of wings.

invisible – unable to be seen.

material – something that other things can be made of, such as fabric, plastic, or metal.

rappel – to climb down the side of a building or mountain by sliding down a rope.

strap – a strip of leather, cloth, or plastic that keeps something tied on.

suspect – a person who is thought to have committed a crime.

tactics – plans for how to win a battle or reach a goal.

violent – likely to attack or hurt others.

waist – the area of your body between your chest and hips.